W9-BLW-460

Behind the Scenes!!

Behind the Scenes!!

06

STORY AND ART BY **BISCO HATORI**

Behind the Scenes!!

06

CONTENTS

SCENE 28 — 5

SCENE 29 — 35

SCENE 30 — 65

SCENE 31 — 95

SCENE 32 — 125

SCENE 33 — 155

BONUS MANGA SCI-FI CLUB!! — 185

GLOSSARY — 188

SCENE 28
Behind the Scenes!!

Behind the Scenes!! 6

Once, there was a bronze statue of a prince that felt pity and love.
He said to his friend the swallow, "Take my gems and give them to the poor."
The swallow took flight many times...
...but when the statue no longer sparkled, the townsfolk forgot him.
Then the angels, who had seen all...
...carried the souls of the prince and swallow to heaven...
...where they dwelled joyfully in the presence of God.

gleam gleam
gleam
gleam
I hope the children enjoy it!
That's the story!
The Happy Prince
ON CHRISTMAS EVE, HUH?
THE ART SQUAD HAS AGREED TO HELP...
...WITH A PUPPET SHOW AT A CHILDREN'S CENTER.
Shichikoku Children's Center

Christmas Party!!
December 24, 9 p.m.
Enjoy a puppet show!!
The Happy
THE CHILDREN MIGHT CRY.
IT'S SO SAD...
WILL THAT BE OKAY?
WAH
GWAH
ON CHRISTMAS EVE?
THERE'S GOTTA BE A MORE APPROPRIATE STORY...
KYAH
YOU MUST BE SOH'S LITTLE BROTHER RIKU!
Hi there!
WELL, THE CENTER WANTS THEM TO HELP.
RAAH
ARE WE GETTING PAID ENOUGH TO SPEND TEN DAYS WITH THESE DEMONS?!
I'M THE ONE WHO'S GONNA CRY!
"HAVE YOU BEEN A BAD BOY?"
THEN HE SLAYS THE INIQUITOUS WITH HIS SCYTHE!
LIKE ABOUT AN OLD MAN DRESSED IN RED WHO...
YES, AND SANTA SAYS...
I KNOW THAT ONE! THAT'S SANTA!

NOOOOO
GYAH
WAAAAAAH
CHRIST-MAS! 'TIS THE SEASON FOR HORROR FLICKS!
SANTA'S RED IS THE RED OF BLOOD!
NOT APPRO-PRIATE! NOT APPRO-PRIATE AT ALL!
Mwaha
ha
IF THE ANGELS WERE WATCHING, WHY DIDN'T THEY ACT SOONER?
WHY WAIT?
mumble mumble
OR A FAMILY IS TAKING A CHRISTMAS DRIVE WHEN A WOMAN IN WHITE APPEARS AND...
MAASA! GODA!
STOP NITPICK-ING!
C'MON, LET'S DIVIDE UP THE WORK.
...ARE MOSTLY OF A COLD FISHING TOWN...
...WITH ONE LITTLE TREE.
WE NEED TO MAKE PUPPETS.
RUKA, YOU'RE IN CHARGE OF THAT.
MY CHRISTMAS MEMORIES ...
Puppet

BUT...
...THIS WHOLE TOWN POSITIVELY GLOWS!
RANMARU!
THERE'S A FABRIC SALE!
RAN-MARU, HOLD THESE!
THERE'S MORE GOODIES OVER THERE!
O...
OKAY!
Kyaah
DUMP WHUMP
FUMP
OOH! BUTTON SETS!
ONE PER PERSON!
Y...
YEAH!
Leftovers Sale
Hobby Store
I'M SHOPPING ALL ALONE WITH RUKA!!
SHE'S SO CUTE WHEN SHE'S HOUSE-WIFEY!
Sh-
If I buy both, can I get a discount?
And a freebie?
Grilled sweet pota-toes!
Sweet Potato
Shinkoku's specialty!
HEART-STRUCK

Puff
SORRY!
THAT VENDOR IS HARD TO CATCH!
Puff
Kyah
Sweet Potatoes
RUKA! BUY THESE FIRST!
HEY, POTATO GUY!
WANT HALF?
IT'S OUR SECRET, OKAY? ☆
I'M SO HAPPY.
I can't bear to eat it!
WAAAH
I WANT THIS MOMENT TO LAST.
Delicious!
Shichikoku Children's Center

General Supervis
Goda
Child Director
Soh Samura
Sets
Maasa
Puppets
Ruka
Eep
Is that Riku's sister?!
Is it?! Really?!
WE'LL DETERMINE ROLES BY LOTTERY.
EVERYONE DO YOUR BEST, OKAY?
H-HEY!
UM, BUT...
Play with us
Yay! Riku's sister!
Ah ha ha...
Okaaay!
Gasp
YOU'RE QUITE A BIG SISTER!
By acci-dent!
I TREATED THEM LIKE RIKU!
GRAH
IF YOU UNDER-STAND, THEN ANSWER!
OR YOU'LL RUIN THE PLAY!
LISTEN TO THE INSTRUC-TIONS!

IT WAS KIND OF YOU TO GET US THIS JOB...
...AND TO HELP OUT.
COME TO THE CHRISTMAS PARTY WITH US!
"WITH US"...
"OUR SECRET" ...
blush
YOU TWO ARE SO OBVIOUS.
What happened ?!

WE HELPED A HIGH SCHOOL DRAMA CLUB...
Heh heh
...AND LEARNED THE VALUE OF NEVER GIVING UP.
FUMP
WOW ---
...MORE BOOKS ?!
Horror Film Handbook
Lessons in Cinema
How to Watch Movies
Russian Animation
The Fundamentals of Anime
The Complete Guide to European Film

Really Scary HORROR Movie
...I borrowed this too!
EEP...
Y-YEAH ...
I HAVE A LOT TO LEARN.
AND, UM...
N...
NO WAY! I'LL NEVER GO OUTSIDE AT NIGHT AGAIN!
BUT I HEARD THAT FEAR ...
Yikes
Yikes
Yikes
...AND BEAUTY ARE INTER-TWINED!
LOTS OF DIRECTORS WHO ARE FAMOUS FOR THEIR GORGEOUS STYLE STARTED IN HORROR!
HORROR HAS AESTHETICS, IMAGINATION AND FETISHISM!
Seri-ously?!
YOU SHOULDN'T CLOSE YOUR EYES WHEN YOU GET SCARED ...
...EVEN IF THE ROAD IS HARSH ...
...OR YOU DON'T STAND A CHANCE.
THAT'S MY GOAL, SO—
FINE! I'LL WATCH IT!
HUH?!

B-BUT ...
NO, REALLY! I NEED CONFIDENCE!
BUT HORROR HAS NOTHING TO DO WITH IZUMI !!
I NEED TO BUILD UP MY STRENGTH ...
...BECAUSE IT'LL BE HARD TO PULL HIS HEAD OUT OF THE CLOUDS.
SO...
...I NEED TO BE A WOMAN WORTH LIKING!
Eeeeek! It really is scary!
Eeeeek!
Eeeeek!
AFTER YOU TAKE ONE STEP FORWARD ...
...IT'S TIME FOR ANOTHER STEP.
AT CHRISTMAS IN THE GIRLS' DORM...

"GET OUT OF THE DORM!"
THE POLICE TRACE THE CALLS AND TELL THE GIRLS...
...AND ONE BY ONE THE GIRLS MEET GRISLY DEATHS.
...A MYSTERIOUS MAN KEEPS CALLING ON THE PHONE...
PRRR

HMM ---
G-GODA?
It...
IT'S GREAT, ISN'T IT!
MAYBE WE CAN TRY THAT!
Or something...
And Michel Ocelot!
ME TOO!
LIKE LOTTE REINIGER AND KAZU-GORO ARAI!
I LIKE IT.
I WAS THINKING ABOUT A SIMPLE POP STYLE, BUT...
SET TEAM! MAASA!
Okay, we need to make frames!
ONE STEP...
...AFTER ANOTHER.
Yay
blah blah
Yay
OH...
--- YOU'RE GETTING ALONG WITH YOUR CLASS-MATES?

I WAS SUR-PRISED ...
...BY YOUR PERFOR-MANCE.
OH, THAT'S GOOD.
Y-YEAH.
A LITTLE BETTER, ANYWAY.
You looked great, Soh!
The play was awe-some!
GRAAAH!
Uwaah!
Yay! Defeat the monster Noppo!
Pile on!!
W-WELL, IT WAS JUST TIRED AND...
SIMPLY PLIT...
HUH?
...WHY DID THE SWALLOW DIE?
Oh! An exca-vation?
Izumi!!
Kyah! Kyah!
One of his 108 hobbies: digging for stuff
UM...
The Happy

Greetings

I made it to volume 6 of *Behind the Scenes!!*

For this volume, I went metal-working!

At Forêt's steampunk jewelry studio...

I played with their dog Watson.

Watson watched as I tinkered away.

I sucked and needed help.

Thanks for your cooperation!!

It was fun!!

THAT'S RIGHT.
ONLY THE SWALLOW COULD HEAR THE PRINCE'S VOICE.
THE PRINCE WAS GLAD TO HAVE EMOTIONS...
...THAT LET HIM HELP THE PEOPLE.
THAT WAS ENOUGH TO MAKE HIM HAPPY.
Ohhhhh...
SHE'S SUCH A SWEET SOUL...
RUKA AND IZUMI...
...ARE SIMILAR.
G...
GUESS WHAT?
IZUMI SAID HE ONLY HAS TEN OUTFITS.
Buys long-sleeved T's on sale three at a time

They find every little thing adorable.
R-Ruka haggles over every yen!
And she eats potato skin!
That's so ador-able!!!
Ah ha ha!
BECAUSE HE'S EVEN KIND TO THE EARTH?
THAT MUST BE IT!
H...
HE DOES?
Y...
YEAH. MAASA SAID HE STOCKS UP AND ROTATES THEM.
BOOKS
Seitendo
ANYWAY, THAT'S WHAT RANMARU SAID.
THAT RUKA AND ME ARE ALIKE?
WE ARE OFTEN IN SYNC, BUT...
THIS IS LIKE A DREAM!

WE'RE WALKING THROUGH TOWN TOGETHER !!
It's so wonderful- how is it going to go wrong?!
LET'S SEE... MARKERS, GLUE...
...AND TOMU WANTS GUMMIES.
Just shopping
BUT ... IZUMI ONCE SAID ...
"YOU SHOULDA CHOSEN ME, BABE..."
"I'D TREAT YA RIGHT!"
Uh... UM...
Are... ARE YOU AND RUKA...
...UM ...
HUH ?
Why do you ask?
NO, NO!
Phew!
TH-THEN ARE THE CHIEF AND RUKA...
RYUJI ?
RYUJI AND RUKA...

Shichikuba Children's Center
THERE! ALL DONE!
IS THIS PATTERN ALL RIGHT?
Huh ?!
WHERE'S RUKA?
NO, SO...
MY FATHER TOLD YOU...
PLEASE, STOP CALLING ME.
YES. I'M SORRY.
NO.
I DOUBT THAT WILL HAPPEN.

Sigh
RANMARU?
UM...
...THE PATTERN'S DONE.
OH, YOU FINISHED?
LEMME SEE!
OOH! I LIKE IT!
Good work!!
UM, ARE YOU ALL RIGHT?
IS THERE A PROBLEM?
HM? NO, I'M FINE!
UH...
HA HA HA!
THAT PHONE CALL?
I WAS TURNING DOWN...
...A PROSPECTIVE PARTNER FOR AN ARRANGED MARRIAGE.

HUH?
MY AUNT ASKED ME TO MEET HER AT A RESTAURANT...
...AND THERE HE WAS! CAN YOU BELIEVE THAT?
I TOLD HER TO WAIT UNTIL AFTER COLLEGE!
AFTER ...
... COLLEGE ?
I'M FROM AN OLD, TRADITIONAL FAMILY...

...SO I HAVE TO GET MARRIED SOON AFTER GRADUATION.
UM, DOES RUKA LIKE ANY—
HM?
LOOK!
THERE'S SANTA!
HE'S HANDING OUT SOME-THING!
HO HO HO! WHAT A NICE COUPLE!

HAVE A COOKIE! IT'S FROM A NEW CAFÉ OPENING THIS CHRISTMAS! ☆
COME CHECK IT OUT!
"C-COUPLE"?!
IT'S A YOUNG GUY IN A COSTUME ...
I CAN TELL FROM HIS VOICE.
MUST BE A YOUNG GUY...
UM...
...SAMURA?!
IZUMI SAMURA? FROM SHII ELEMENTARY?

IT'S ME! OKANO!
DON'T YOU REMEMBER? WE WERE IN FIFTH AND SIXTH GRADE TOGETHER!
I MOVED FOR JUNIOR HIGH, SO IT'S BEEN NINE YEARS!
DO YOU GO TO UNIVERSITY AROUND HERE?
UM...
HUH? DON'T YOU RECOGNIZE ME?
WE ALWAYS WENT TO AZARASHI PARK TOGETHER!
A GIANT DOG LIVED NEAR THERE ---
---AND YOU INSISTED IT WAS A POLAR BEAR!
SORRY...

...I DON'T REMEM-BER.
OH...
...
THEN, UH...
Sorry to bother you.
DON'T LOOK SO SAD.

I CAN'T DO ANY-THING ABOUT IT.
MY PARENTS PROMISED TO WAIT UNTIL AFTER COLLEGE ...
...AND LET ME CHOOSE WHERE TO ATTEND.
THEY WERE AGAINST ME JOINING THE ART SQUAD...
...BUT EVENTU-ALLY I CONVINCED THEM.
I CAN'T DO ANY-THING ABOUT IT.

AND THAT'S ENOUGH.
I'M ACTUALLY QUITE HAPPY!
BUT...
...THEN...
...WHAT ABOUT GODA?
"THE PRINCE WAS GLAD TO HAVE EMOTIONS ..."

"THAT WAS ENOUGH TO MAKE HIM HAPPY."
"SOME THINGS ARE JUST INEVITABLE."

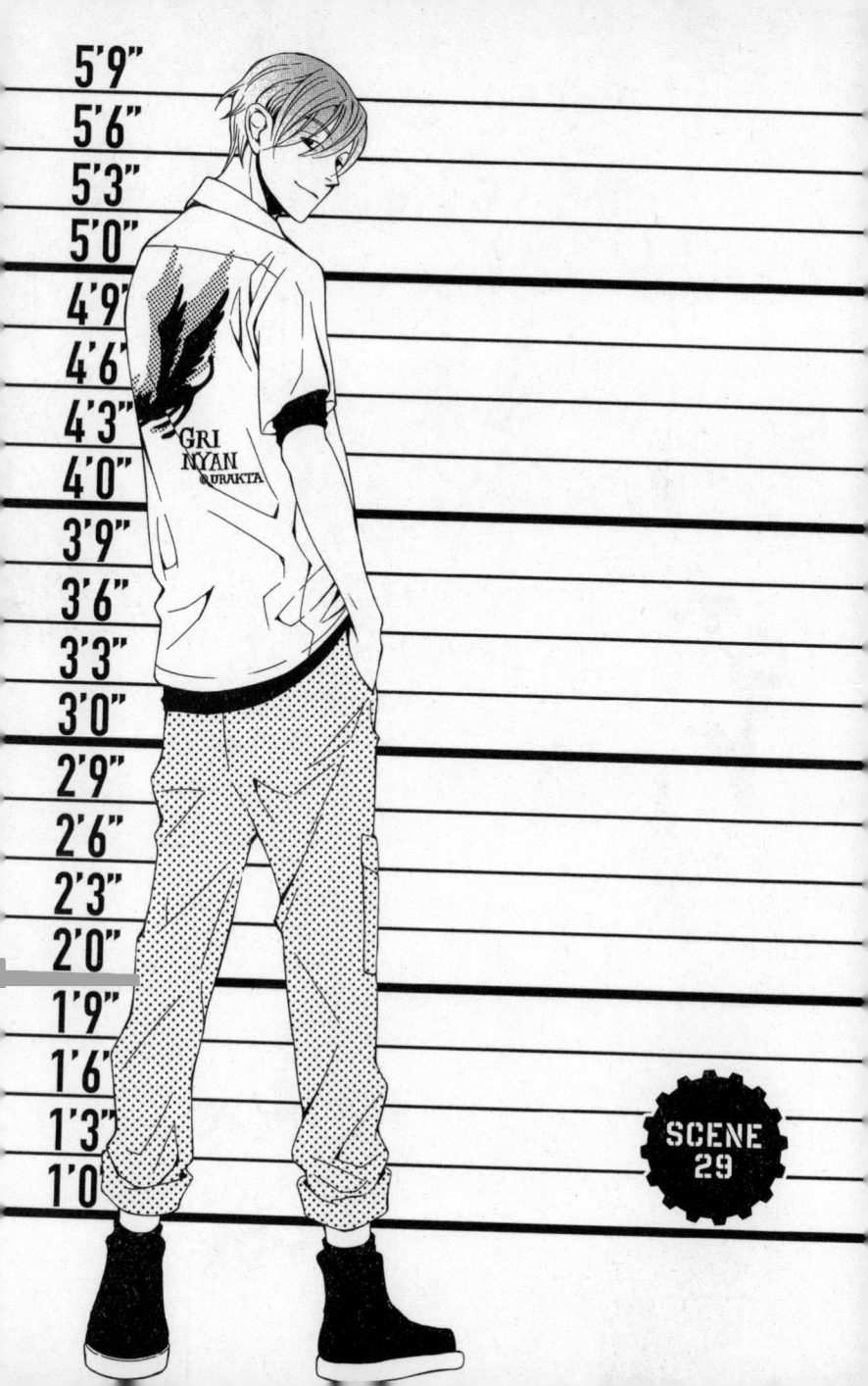
5'9"
5'6"
5'3"
5'0"
4'9"
4'6"
4'3"
4'0"
3'9"
3'6"
3'3"
3'0"
2'9"
2'6"
2'3"
2'0"
1'9"
1'6"
1'3"
1'0"
GRI
NYAN
©URAKTA
SCENE
29

WE RE-SOLVED NEVER TO GIVE UP...
I CAN'T DO ANYTHING ABOUT IT.
...AND GAINED THE COURAGE TO MOVE FORWARD ...
I CAN'T DO ANYTHING ABOUT IT.
Y...
...BUT...
YOU MUSTN'T GIVE UP!

M...
MAYBE I CAN HELP YOU!
I KNOW I'M BASICALLY NOBODY, BUT...
... BUT ...
NO-BODY ?
BUT I...
I LIKE Y—
What was I saying ?!
WELL, SHALL WE GO...
...SOH?
TA DAH
I'M JOINING THE SHOPPING EXPEDI-TION!!
THE CHIEF'S GOT A CRAVING FOR DRIED PLUMS!
OH, OKAY.

SORRY.
Case 1
Izumi
HE'S SUFFERING FROM AMNESIA DUE TO THE ACCIDENT.
I CAN'T SAY IF HE'LL EVER REGAIN HIS MEMORY.

WHO AM I? WHERE AM I?
I FEEL LIKE I'VE HEARD THOSE PHRASES BEFORE...
...BUT I DON'T REMEMBER WHEN OR WHERE.
IZUMI!
BIG BRO!!
YOU ALL RIGHT, SAMURA?
I SAW MY FAMILY AND FRIENDS AGAIN FOR THE FIRST TIME.
YOU DON'T REMEMBER ANYTHING?
I RECORDED NEW MEMORIES IN A BLANK NOTEBOOK...
IZUMI...
...DID YOU REMEMBER SOMETHING?
...BUT MY SENSE OF GUILT...
...WAS A HOLLOW SPACE I COULD NEVER FILL.

I FEEL HEAVY... SO HEAVY...
BUT THEN ONE DAY I REALIZED ...
I CAN'T DO ANY-THING ABOUT IT.
PO
mf
Case 2 Ruka
I'M WORRIED ABOUT RUKA.
SHE'S GOOD AT DESIGNING CLOTHES, BUT THAT ISN'T PRACTICAL FOR HOME-MAKING.
I'M FROM A FAMILY OF DOCTORS ...
...BUT I DIDN'T INHERIT ANY APTITUDE FOR MEDICINE.
Oh, well...
SOME OF MY COUSINS HAVE EXCELLED ...
...SO MAYBE I CAN LEAVE SOMEDAY.
ALL SUCH THOUGHTS OF FREE-DOM...

...ENDED WITH MY MOTHER'S DEATH.
I'M YOUR NEW MOTHER!
WILL HIS SECOND WIFE RAISE HER PROPERLY?
EITHER WAY, RUKA'S IN HER HANDS NOW.
Klank
UH-OH...
IT'S TOO LATE TO ESCAPE!
I WEPT AND STRUGGLED...
...BUT THEN I REALIZED ...
I CAN'T DO ANYTHING ABOUT IT.
I can't break free!
OH, I GET IT...
RUKA GAVE UP...

...TO ESCAPE DESPERATION.
SOMETIMES ACCEPTING CIRCUM-STANCES...
I can't believe I told you!
STOP LOAFING, YOU TWO!
...OFFERS A RAY OF LIGHT...
...THAT ILLUMINATES A PATH FORWARD.
TA
The Happy Prince
LOOK WHAT THE SET TEAM MADE!!
DAH

Wow! Coool!
The Happy Prince
Yeah!
AND WHEN YOU PULL THIS CORD...
KYAAH! IT'S WONDER-FUL!!
SH
UNK
The Happy Prince
Huh?!
NEXT YEAR, YOU GOTTA DO BETTER ON YOUR OWN!
YO, PUNKS!
SHUNK SHUNK
Heh heh!
AND IF YOU TURN THIS HANDLE ...
WOW!! THE BACK-GROUND CHANGES !!
No, you must learn to strive!!
That's impos-sible !!
I CAN'T SAY ANY-THING.

GRAH GRAH
IT JUST ISN'T ME.
IT MAKES ME SO HAPPY TO LOOK AT THIS!
I'M NOT THE ONE...
What's all the excite-ment?
We're Back!
...SHE GAZES AT SO INTENTLY.

Whoa! What's this?! Cool!
tug
HE TURNED ME DOWN.
"I'M SORRY."
"I CAN'T RETURN YOUR FEELINGS."
"I THINK ...
...I'M INCAPABLE OF LOVING ANYONE."

DON'T CRY.
I MUSTN'T CRY.
WHEN I THINK ABOUT THOSE TWO...
Oh! Snow!
See ya tomorrow!
...I CAN'T HELP BUT WISH...

...THAT I WERE THE ONE BY HER SIDE.
RAN-MARU !!
ONLY FOUR DAYS TO GO!
ARE THE PUPPETS READY?
Shichikoku Children's Center

DA DUM
WHAT'S WITH THE GLASSES ??
Cosplay?
Um... Uh...
W...
WE'VE GOT ALLERGIES THAT IRRITATE OUR EYES...
AND THE CHILDREN'S REHEARSALS ARE GOING WELL!!
Script
Y...
YES! ALMOST !!
SOH, CAN YOU HELP THE SWALLOW WITH HIS LINES?
N...
NO STRIVING! JUST LET IT GO!
Cypress? Ragweed?
I HAVE HEARD OF WINTER ALLERGIES...
Oh?!
HOW INTERESTING ...
YEAH, I'M SUPER STOKED !!
ba bing
AH HA HA! THAT'S THE SPIRIT!
YEAH, SURE !!
AND MAY I HELP?
ba bmp

Let's Watch Movies! ①
Dear readers...
Do you have an aversion to certain movie genres?
I sure do.
Horror
Violence
SPLATTER
Flesh
Anything scary...
On a related topic...
...I have difficulty understanding old movies.
...the tempo...
Like...
But...
For many years...
...I've thought scary movies looked interesting.
(I've always loved mysteries.)
Seven
Silence of the Lambs
Psycho
It'd be great if I understood old masterpieces!
bloop
ALL NIGHT...
THANK YOU.
...WE CRIED AND CRIED.
UNABLE TO DO ANYTHING ELSE...
...WE DECIDED TO JUST KEEP DOING OUR BEST.
Soh, your eyes are red!!
Yours too!!

OH...
...YOU WANT TO BE A BASE-BALL PLAYER, AI?
WOW!
I'M GONNA PITCH A NO-HITTER AT KOSHIEN !!
Yep!!
No way!
GIRLS CAN'T PLAY AT KOSHIEN!
CAN TOO!!
I'm gonna go to Koshien!
WELL, THERE'S GIRLS' BASEBALL TOO, SO...
Maybe that's better?
Ko-shi-en!!
No ooo!
DON'T BE SO CERTAIN, GUYS!
ARE YOU SURE MARTIANS WON'T INVADE TOMOR-ROW?
GRAAAH
OR THAT YOU WON'T SUD-DENLY WARP TO ANOTHER WORLD WHERE THE LOCALS WORSHIP YOU AS THEIR SAVIOR?!
Huh?!
COOL!! I WANNA BE A HERO!!
MAYBE SOMEDAY GIRLS WILL PLAY AT KOSHIEN.
YOU NEVER KNOW WHAT WILL HAPPEN.

TH-THAT'S RIGHT!
Good luck, Ai!!
Thanks!
...
VERY GOOD, RIKU!
I can't wait for the puppet show!
Hm?
BUT...
Look!
Sis!!
I drawed the prince and birdie!!
HAPPY PRINCE
...DIDN'T YOU SAY THE STORY MAKES YOU SAD?
The other day...
BUT THEN I HAD AN IDEA!!
THE PRINCE HELPS POOR PEOPLE, RIGHT?
"THAT WAS ENOUGH TO MAKE HIM HAPPY."
BUT...

...SOMETHING ELSE MADE HIM HAPPY TOO!!
WE BELIEVED...
HUH?
...WE WERE POWERLESS TO DO ANYTHING.

WHY'RE YOU TWO HERE SO LATE?
G...
GODA ---
...WE HAVE A SUGGES-TION!!
What gives?!
IT'S TOO LATE ---
...FOR A MAIDEN LIKE ME TO BE OUT!
You rang?!

Oh...
HELP US OUT HERE.
IT'LL BE HARD TO ACCOMPLISH IN THREE DAYS...
...BUT STICKING TO THE PLAN IS BORING!
Shichikoku Children's
CHRISTMAS
IZUMI !!

HAPPY PRINCE
IT'S SO BOISTEROUS IN HERE!
chatter
chatter
GODA DIDN'T INCLUDE YOU EITHER ?
ISN'T HE MEAN?!
Ah ha ha!
WHAT'S HE PLOTTING?
HEY, DID YOU...
...MAKE SOH CRY?
ULP...
BUT...
...IT'S STRANGE.
SHE'S THE FIRST SINCERE GIRL TO DO THAT.
FAITHFUL SWALLOW ...

...GIVE MY GEMS TO THE PEOPLE!
AT THE DILAPI-DATED PRINCE'S FEET...
...THE SWALLOW LAY DOWN FOREVER ...
bl oo op
Or so it seemed !!!

Clank!
Clank!
KAZAMM
SUD-DENLY, A BRIGHT LIGHT ZAPPED THEM!
BWO
Super Prince of Good Fortune!!!
Mega-Strong Combo!
OSH
WHAA AAT ?!
THE PRINCE AND SWALLOW CAME BACK AS ROBOTS !!!

ALL THE TOWNS-FOLK APPLAUDED ---
...AND SHOUTED THEIR PRAISE!
THREE CHEERS FOR THE PRINCE!
HURRAH!!
HURRAH!!
HURRAH!!
Bwa ha

Ah
I didn't see THAT coming!
ha
ha
ha
ha
ha
YES...
...NO ONE KNOWS HOW THE STORY WILL END.
cinema

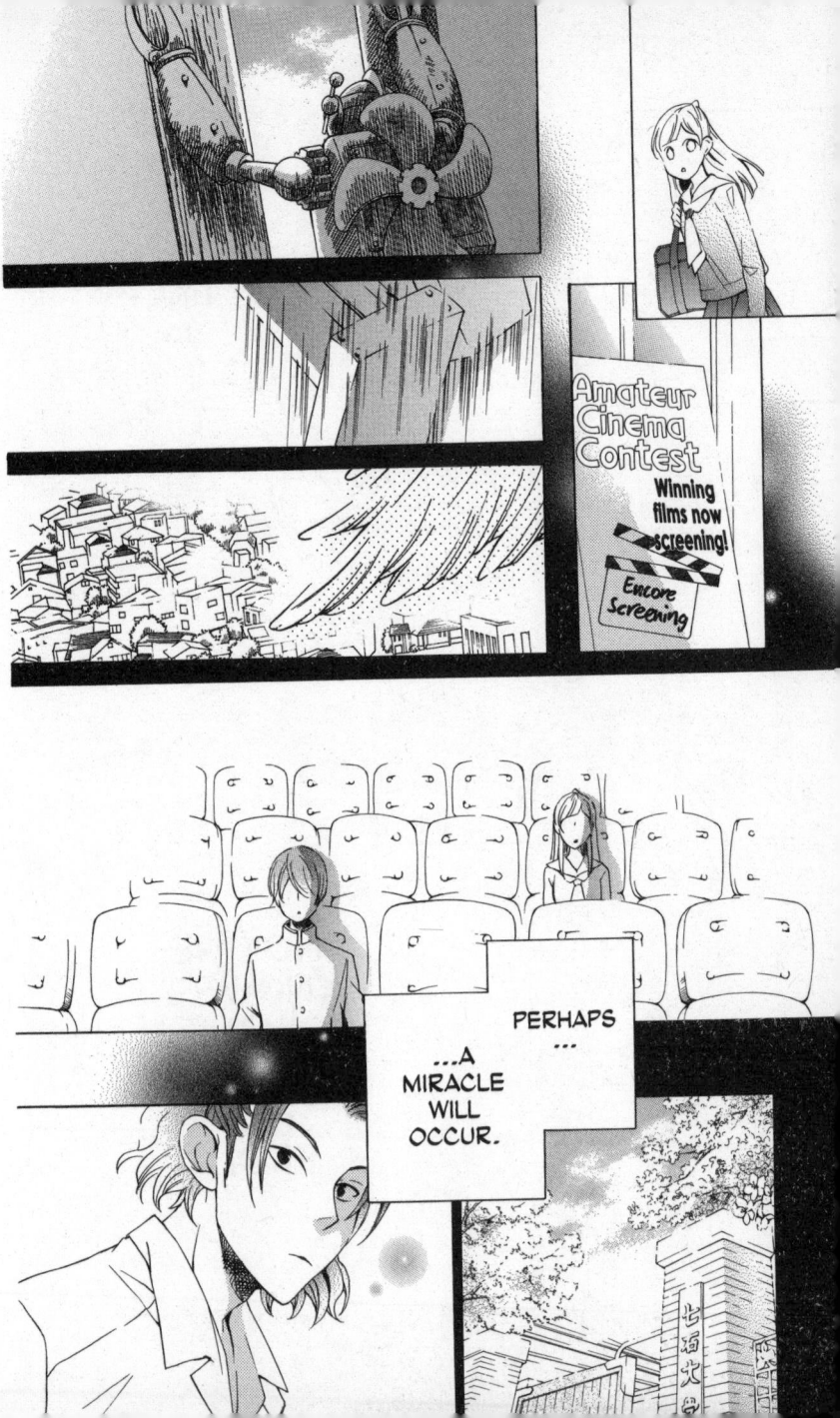
Amateur Cinema Contest
Winning films now screening!
Encore Screening
PERHAPS ...
...A MIRACLE WILL OCCUR.

SO RIGHT HERE AND NOW...
...LAUGH WITH OTHERS AS much AS YOU CAN.
The Happy Prince
THE PRINCE WAS HAPPY...
...BECAUSE HE WASN'T ALONE!

HE HAD A GOOD FRIEND!
THUS, THE CURTAIN FELL ON CHRISTMAS IN MY FIRST YEAR OF COLLEGE.

WAIT! WAIT!
WHY DON'T COLLEGES HAVE UNIFORMS ?!
SOH! I'M GOING!
I NEVER KNOW WHAT TO WEAR!
YOU'RE COMING WITH ME PARTWAY, AREN'T YOU?

HM?
DID YOU GET TALLER?
I DON'T KNOW.
A GROWTH SPURT? AT THIS AGE?
I'M IN MY SECOND YEAR NOW!
Ahhahaha!
MAYBE A FRESHMAN WILL POUR HER HEART OUT TO YOU!
YEAH, I DOUBT THAT.

5'9"
5'6"
5'3"
5'0"
4'9"
4'6"
4'3"
4'0"
3'9"
3'6"
3'3"
3'0"
2'9"
2'6"
2'3"
2'0
1'9"
1'6
1'3"
1'0"
SCENE
30

TA-
SPRING HAS COME!!
DUM
Shichikoku U. Baseball
Recruiting!
Let's go!
Theater Studies
Enjoy Cheer Band
Rainb
Shichikoku U. Cheerleading
Ski Circle
Dolphi
Karate Club
Shichikoku U. Railway Study
Walking
SURVIVAL GAMES
Shichikoku
SURVIVAL
Anime Studies
Rugby Club
Freshmen Welcome
Shichikoku University

Basketball players are babe magnets!
Gyaah
'O sole mio!
Join American football!
Waah
Join calligraphy!
Drama
IT'S THE TIME OF YEAR FOR ~~HARVESTING~~ RECRUITING NEW CLUB MEMBERS!!
Film Studies Orientation & Welcome
I WOULD LIKE...
...ALL PROSPECTIVE MEMBERS TO MAKE A TEN-MINUTE FILM.
SENIOR CLUB MEMBERS AND THE ART SQUAD WILL HELP YOU.
YOU NEED TO TRY MAKING A FILM...
...TO GET A FEEL FOR THE CLUB.

Noo!
I'm not a new student!
Come with us, froshie!!
Yesterday
Art Squad
YOU'VE GOT A FRESH SECOND-YEAR STUDENT ...
...SO I THOUGHT YOU DIDN'T NEED NEW ONES.
S...
Yeah...
WE DO HAVE AN IDIOT LIKE THAT!
WE HAVE 15 NEW MEMBERS.
AND YOU DON'T HAVE ANY?
WE'RE LATE-BLOOMERS.
REALLY?
SORRY! I DON'T LOOK MY AGE!
BUT YOU HAVE GROWN.
ANYWAY, THERE'S STILL TIME!
YEAH, THIS IS OUR CHANCE TO SNAG RECRUITS!
Mwa ha ha...
MORE MEMBERS, MORE POWER!
AND MORE TIME FOR ME TO HIT SINGLES' PARTIES!!
GW
AND MORE MEMBER DUES!!
AH

EXCUSE ME.
WHAT KIND OF EQUIPMENT DO YOU HAVE?
AND YOU ARE?
Welcome!
I WANT MY NEXT FILM TO BE IN 4K.
AND I WANT A SINGLE-FOCUS LENS INSTEAD OF A ZOOM LENS.
MIHARU HANEIKE. ECO-NOMICS, YEAR 1.
AND POST-PRODUCTION IS IMPORTANT, SO I'LL NEED SOUND EDITING AND EDITING STAFF.
HANEIKE... I KNOW THAT NAME...
OH!

AEC
AMATEUR CINEMA CONTEST
Amateur Cinema Contest
Top > Archive > Winners > Director
Fall 2013
Tumble 2014
Miharu Haneike
LOOK !!
HE WON THE AMATEUR CINEMA CONTEST TWO YEARS IN A ROW!!

...BUT I HEARD THIS CLUB IS FAIRLY ACTIVE.
MY HIGH SCHOOL DIDN'T HAVE A FILM CLUB, SO I WAS UNDER-STAFFED ...
Film
Welcome!
IN HIS LAST YEAR OF JUNIOR HIGH AND FIRST YEAR OF HIGH SCHOOL ?

Heh
THE NEW KID...
...FROM YOU UPPER-CLASS-MEN!
SO I EXPECT A LOT...

...IS A FORCE TO BE RECKONED WITH!!
FOR ...
...A SENSE OF SPEED, I'LL NEED TO BLOCK A LOT OF CAMERAS.
BUT THAT'S TIME-CONSUMING, SO...
There are other students too.
THEN GET MORE CAMERAS.
But...
WE DON'T HAVE THOSE KINDS OF RE-SOURCES!
SO I'M SUP-POSED TO CUT CORNERS?
Sigh
THAT WILL ONLY RESULT IN A THIRD-RATE FILM!
SNAP

ARE THE EGGS READY?
UH, YES.
HEY, RAN-MARU?
GRAR
Uh-oh!
Fine! You can have 100! Or 200!!
Stubborn pride
Use a tack or needle to start a hole.
Then widen it with a drill.
THEY'RE FILMING FROM FIVE ANGLES, SO I MADE A DOZEN.
I DRILLED HOLES, DRAINED THEM...
...AND FILLED THEM WITH RED LIQUID.
There's a woman...
...who breaks them...
...one after the other...
Raw egg on rice! Yum!
The talented rookie Haneike had a vision...
I'm worried...
WILL THIS REALLY WORK?

...as if possessed ...
...and driven to extremity.
SPLAA
ATT
CUT !!
Gah! That's gross!

HOW DO YOU MAKE THEM STAND UP?
Um...
I TRIED DIFFERENT THINGS, BUT KNEADED ERASER WORKS BEST.
OKAY!
I'LL SET UP THE EGGS!
NOW ...
...A SHOT FROM ABOVE THE EGGS.
I'M IN A HURRY, SO SET THEM UP AND CLEAR OUT!
Eep!
S-SORRY!
WAS MY PERFORMANCE ALL RIGHT?
Do you have any notes for me?
Film Studies
What's with him?!
I'LL FILM IT SO IT LOOKS GOOD...
...NO MATTER HOW MUCH YOUR ACTING REEKS.
WHAT?!
HE HAS AN IMPRESSIVE BACKGROUND ...
...BUT HIS PERSONALITY BITES.

CHIEF, SAY SOME-THING!
Are you gonna let that slide?!
GOOD FILMS DON'T REQUIRE GOOD PERSON-ALITIES.
AFTER ALL, CONSIDER THE OTHER GUYS.
Point taken.
UGH
Quirky
CUT!! IT STILL LACKS IMPACT !!
AND HOLD THE CAMERA STILL!
AND THE PANNING IS OUT OF SYNC!
AGAIN!
AGAIN!!
AGAIN !!!
BUT I'M OUT OF EGGS !!!
TOMU! SUPER-MARKET DASH!!
Aye, aye, sir!!

UM, I THINK IT'S GOOD ENOUGH, SO...
THAT'S BECAUSE YOU DON'T HAVE AN EYE FOR CINEMA.
Chomp
Argh
If he wasn't talented, I'd strangle him!
It needs more impact...
mutter
mutter
mutter

OH DEAR ...

...HE SOUNDS SCARY.

BUT THEY SAY HE'S TALENTED.
HMM ---
THEN HE SHOULD GO TO FILM SCHOOL!
Or join the film department!
Yeah!!
SPSHH
HAVE YOU JOINED A CLUB, SOH?
TENNIS?
NO...
...I'M CONSIDERING THE DRAMA CLUB.
Huh?! As an actress ?!
Because of your recent performance?
N...
NO, I'LL WORK BEHIND THE SCENES.
HELPING THE DRAMA CLUB WAS FUN.
BESIDES ---

...I WANT ...
...TO STAY CLOSE TO HIM.
...
SHE'S STILL...
...NOT OVER IZUMI.
WE CRY AND SPIN OUR WHEELS ...
HE'S DOING WELL.
How about you? You see those two all the time...
Ugh. Don't remind me!
COME VISIT SOME-TIME!
...AND STRUGGLE TO OVER-COME.
OKAY ...

tak
tak
AND WE LEARN SOME-THING EVERY DAY.
AEC Amateur Cin
Miharu Haneike
Gondaira Nanas
YEAH... NOT BAD...

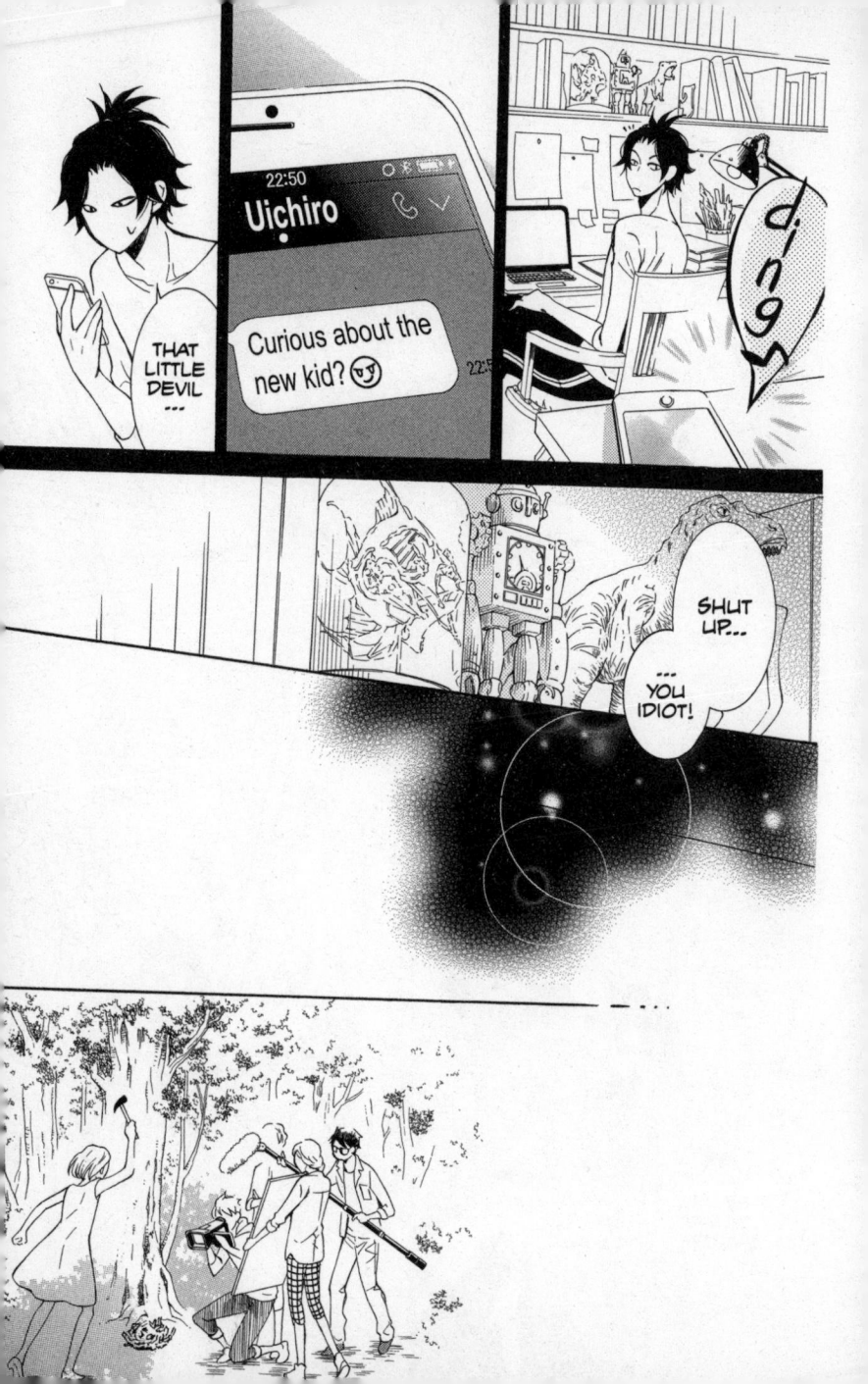
THAT LITTLE DEVIL ...
22:50
Uichiro
Curious about the new kid? 😈
ding
SHUT UP...
... YOU IDIOT!

KR
SMP
CUT !!
IT LACKS IMPACT!
SOUND, GET YOUR POSITION RIGHT!!
We're running out of bird nests!
She breaks...
...and breaks...
...and just keeps breaking...
AND THE CAMERA-WORK IS SLOPPY !!
IF YOU CARE ABOUT THIS, THEN GET IT TOGETHER!
Sigh
WE WON'T FINISH TODAY EITHER.

WHAT'S YOUR IDEAL DIRECTOR LIKE?
A DIRECTOR SHOULD SET THE TONE OF THE PRODUCTION.
I HATE THIS KIND OF DIRECTOR.
LOOK AT EVERYONE'S FACES.
IN OTHER WORDS, A DIRECTOR SHOULD BE DECISIVE AND PERSONABLE.
THE WAY I SEE IT, HORROR SHOULD BE MORE...
mutter
...BUT TOO MUCH IMPACT CAN LACK DEPTH.
I LOVE ME SOME GROTESQUERIE ...
mutter
A DIRECTOR NEEDS VISION.
WHETHER IT'S EXTERNAL SCENERY ...
...OR PORTRAYING INTERNAL STATES ...
...A DIRECTOR MAKES YOU WANT TO SEE THROUGH THEIR EYES.

Gasp
OH, NOTHING!
WHAT GIVES?
Hm? Why was I staring?
Well, stop slacking!
...
A DIRECTOR'S ...
... VISION?
KNOCK IT OFF ALREADY!!
WE AREN'T ROBOTS!
BUT YOU'RE INCOMPETENT. I WAS JUST BEING HONEST.
DON'T TALK TO PEOPLE LIKE THAT!

WELL, IF YOU CAN'T KEEP UP...
WHAT ELSE CAN WE DO?!
ALL YOU TALK ABOUT IS IMPACT!
"I'M DONE WITH THIS!"
"WHAT ELSE CAN WE DO?!"
...THEN JUST LEAVE.
35TH AEC AMATEUR CINEMA CONTEST GRAND PRIX
38TH AEC AMATEUR CINEMA CONTEST GRAND PRIX
I'M GIVING MY ALL.
AEC AMATEUR CINEMA CONTEST
37th Amateur Cinema Contest Result
Rejected
AND THIS ISN'T GOOD ENOUGH!
AEC AMATEUR CINEMA CONTEST
羽池三治 様
38th Amateur Cinema Contest Result
Rejected
IT ISN'T GOOD ENOUGH!
She broke...
...and broke...

...until she broke her-self.
WHAT I HAVE IN MIND IS MORE...
HEY.
PEOPLE CAN'T KEEP UP...
...BECAUSE YOU DON'T LOVE THE FILM.

YOU CAN BE A JERK IF YOU WANT...
I DON'T CARE.
BUT I WON'T HELP SOMEONE WHO DOESN'T KNOW WHAT HE WANTS.
YOU'RE UNDER PRESSURE ...
...AND STRUG-GLING THROUGH A SLUMP ...
"IT'S NO GOOD ..."
"IT NEEDS MORE IMPACT!"
"MORE!"
"MORE!"
...BUT YOU'RE THE ONE WHO ISN'T DOING HIS JOB!

NO ONE WILL ENJOY A MOVIE THAT YOU YOURSELF DON'T LOVE.
NO...
Nanda University Department Guide
Film study
NANDA UNIVERSITY
THAT'S NOT IT...
I...
Music Club
Pep Team
Ski Social Club
Studies
Nanda University

Welcome!
Film Studies Club
I STILL WANT TO MAKE MOVIES!
WE CRY...
...AND SPIN OUR WHEELS ...
...AND STRUGGLE TO OVERCOME.
WHEN DID GODA NOTICE...
... HANEIKE'S ISOLATION AND FRUSTRATION?
GODA ALWAYS SEES DEEP INSIDE PEOPLE.
"A DIRECTOR NEEDS VISION."

I WISH I COULD SEE...
...THROUGH HIS EYES.

LATER...
...HANEIKE OFFICIALLY JOINED FILM STUDIES.
CUT !!
NO !!
JUST QUIT, YOU IDIOT!!
YOU'RE SO INCOM-PETENT!
YEAH...
Tee hee...
What'd you say?!
Another rant? Whatever!
Are you even listening?!
HIS TONGUE IS EVEN SHARPER NOW...
...BUT LOOK!
HE'S HAVING FUN!
You sure about that?
BY THE WAY...

GLOOOM
No membership dues...
No singles' parties...
...THE ART SQUAD NEVER DID GET NEW RECRUITS.
THAT NIGHT...
...I WATCHED A DVD FROM THE LIBRARY.
AEC
Amateur Cinema Contest Selections
HANEIKE'S SHORT FILM...
...REALLY WAS IMPRESSIVE.
THESE ARE THE WINNERS FOR THE LAST TEN YEARS.
I'LL WATCH THE ONE FROM EIGHT YEARS AGO NEXT...
bip

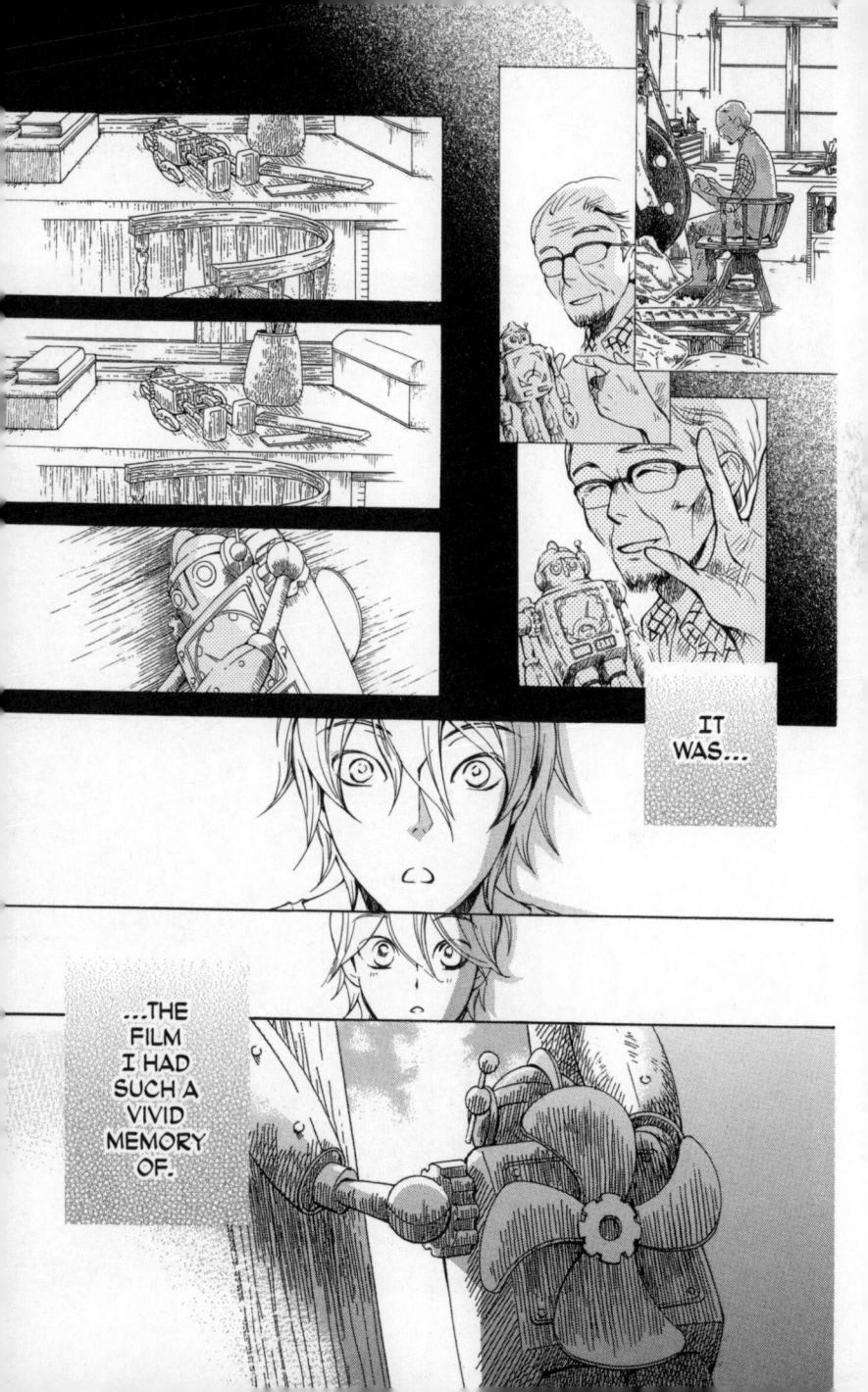
IT WAS...
...THE FILM I HAD SUCH A VIVID MEMORY OF.

Directed by
RYUJI GODA

SCENE
31

THE DIREC-TOR...
...OF THE FILM I HAD SEEN YEARS AGO...
It's a little late, but has anyone noticed that Shichikoku sounds a bit like Hitchcock?
Based on director Michael Haneke.
I want to see *Funny Games*. But it looks scary, so I still haven't...
羽池三治
Miharu Haneike (18)

Directed by
RYUJI GODA
YES, THAT'S RIGHT!
Wimbledon University

HE MADE IT IN THE FIRST YEAR OF JUNIOR HIGH.
HE WAS THE YOUNGEST EVER TO WIN THE GRAND PRIX!
YOU KNEW?
HUH?
WHAT?!
Ah ha ha! YOU FINALLY REALIZED, HUH?
RYUJI MADE THE MOVIE YOU SAW YEARS AGO.
WE HAPPENED TO SEE IT BACK THEN TOO.
I WAS THRILLED ...
...WHEN I MET HIM IN COLLEGE !!
RUKA EVEN ASKED FOR HIS AUTOGRAPH!
YEP! I SURE DID!!
"I'M SURPRISED."

"I DIDN'T KNOW THE CHIEF HAD SUCH SKILLS!!"
"BUT STILL, HOW DO YOU KNOW SO MUCH?"
At summer camp
Huh?
"YOU SHOULD PICK IT UP NATURALLY!"
AH, SO THAT EXPLAINS IT!
Huh? Goda really made that movie? Seriously?
Ah ha ha! He's in shock!
HUH? REALLY?
PANIC
Why is working behind the scenes?
HUH? SO WHY...
...IS HE IN THE ART SQUAD?
WELL ...
...HE DOESN'T LIKE TO TALK...
... ABOUT WHY HE QUIT DIRECTING.
I BET THERE'S A CURSE.
Gyah!

MAASA, DID YOU KNOW ABOUT THAT MOVIE?
NO ...
HE FILMED WHAT SHOULD NOT BE FILMED!
FOR REAL? LIKE A GHOST OR SOME-THING?
AND THEN THE CAMERA BROKE AND...
Yi-i-ikes!!!
M...

Previous instance:
Izumi's memory loss
...SO JUST LIKE USUAL ...
...I'M THE LAST ONE TO KNOW !!
THIS IS BIG! I GOTTA ASK HIM ABOUT IT!
WHERE'S THE CHIEF?
HM ?
Me too!!

Film Studies
Shichikoku Universit
Film Studies

RAN-MARU! TOMU! LET'S GO!
Huh?
TO GODA'S PLACE?
NO! I KNOW SOMEONE WHO CAN GIVE US THE SCOOP!!
IZUMI, HAVE YOU SEEN HIM TODAY ?
NO. DID HE TAKE TODAY OFF?
THAT RAT...
He escaped my clutches!

...I KNOW ALL ABOUT THAT...
YES...
...AND ABOUT THAT TRAITOR.
Film Studies
Uichiro Hida
SURPRISINGLY, WE USED TO BE CLOSE.
WAS IT A CURSE?! HUH?! WAS IT?!
WELL, IF GODA DOESN'T WANT US TO KNOW, THEN...
※Uichiro→
WE BOTH ADORED MOVIES SO MUCH ...
...THAT WE WANTED TO MAKE THEM, NOT JUST WATCH THEM.
WE PROMISED TO BECOME MOVIE DIRECTORS.

TO BE HONEST ...
...HE HAD THE BETTER VISION AND TECHNIQUE, BY FAR.
I WAS JEALOUS AND STRUGGLED TO KEEP UP.
HAVING A FIERCE RIVAL CAN BE INVIGORATING...
...BUT ...
...HE SUDDENLY QUIT...
...SOON AFTER WINNING AN AMATEUR CONTEST.
THAT'S THE MOVIE!
YOU ...
...SAID SOMETHING INTERESTING ...
IT MAY INDEED BE A KIND OF CURSE.
HE WAS STUCK AND COULDN'T CRAWL BACK UP.

CURSED WITH THE INESCAPABLE SIN...
...THAT COMES WITH MAKING A FILM!
WE CAN DISCUSS AT LENGTH ---
Heh
...THE OLD MAN WHO APPEARS IN THAT FILM.
I HAD NO IDEA...

HE'S ALWAYS SO CONFI-DENT.
I WASN'T SUPPOSED TO KNOW ABOUT THIS...
BV
VVT
GODA!
I BROUGHT BEEF BOWLS!
Beef
Wheen
Huff
COOL. GOOD WORK!
SCRATCH
SCRATCH
SCRATCH
Grrrrrowl

Read 20:42
Beef bowl! Urgent! Run!!
SWOOSH
OH, EXTRA-LARGE HELP-INGS!!
Awe-some!!
UM, YOU DON'T FEEL UNWELL?
NOPE! NOT A BIT!
WHEN I GET LOST IN NEW PROJ-ECTS ...
...I SKIP MEALS AND CLASSES.
CHAS-ING?
chomp chomp
Deli-cious!
YEAH.
HE GETS HIS LOVE OF METAL CHASING ...
...FROM HIS GRAND-FATHER.

THERE WAS A TINPLATE FACTORY BEHIND HIS FAMILY'S TEMPLE.
HE COULD MAKE ALL MANNER OF THINGS...
...FROM TINPLATE, AS IF BY MAGIC.
GODA ALWAYS WENT TO WATCH.
BUT ONE DAY, HIS GRAND-FATHER WASN'T THERE.

He wasn't close to his children.
It was his heart.
N-NO, IT'S JUST ...
...I'VE NEVER SEEN THIS STUFF BEFORE.
RAN-MARU?
What's wrong? You hungry?
It's all gone.
Gasp
IS THIS WHAT YOU'RE WORKING ON?

Turbine
Yeah.
I'M INTO MAKING TURBINES.
YOU MAKE A RING AND—
YOU MADE THIS FROM A METAL PLATE?
YEAH. BRASS.
BUT THESE PARTS ARE FROM COPPER-PLATE.
WOW!!
WANNA MAKE SOME-THING?
WHAT ?!
IT'S YOUR FIRST TIME, RIGHT?
SO MAKE A SIMPLE BRASS RING.
With a burner
FIRST, ANNEAL THE BASE METAL ---
...TO MAKE IT MALLEA-BLE.
PWAH
Whoa...
IT TURNED BRIGHT RED!
WHEN THE COLOR CHANGES ---

L... LIKE THIS?
THEN WRAP IT AROUND THIS CORE ROD.
...PLUNGE IT INTO WATER.
THEN YOU CAN SHAPE IT BY HAND.
gwop
SZZZZ
tonk tonk
USE A HAMMER TO BEND IT...
...INTO THE APPROXI-MATE SHAPE.
THEN USE A FRET-SAW TO CUT AWAY EXCESS.
SEE HOW IT'S CURVED?
NOW POUND THE CURVE FLAT.
BAM
OW!
UNTIL YOU GET USED TO IT, THAT'LL HAPPEN.
Keep trying!
Chasing...
BUT WAIT...
...WE'RE JUST GETTING STARTED!

Casting
Forging
Chasing
...is one form of metal-working.
...WHILE CASTING INVOLVES POURING MOLTEN METAL INTO A MOLD.
FORGING INVOLVES HITTING THE METAL INTO SHAPE...
Chasing was once used in decorating swords and armor.
How can we earn a living?
Interesting, huh?
Oh, cool!
...metal-workers began crafting accessories like we have today.
When the Haitorei Edict prohibited weapons...

This surface
IT'S AN ANVIL FOR POUNDING METAL...
...LIKE WHEN STRETCHING SILVER.
tonk
tonk
YOU CAN FLATTEN A VERTICAL PLANE.
WHAT'S THIS BIG THING?
Oh...
THIS IS CALLED A KANADOKO.
gwip
...THEN JOIN THE SOFT AREAS.
PWAHH
ANNEAL AND COOL IT AGAIN...
NEXT IS SOLDERING.
Soldering
YOU USE A METAL THAT LIQUIFIES AT A LOWER TEMPERATURE THAN BRASS...
tss
tss
...SO THE METAL SERVES AS GLUE.
PWAH
If the edges don't match, use the fretsaw.
GRND
GRND
NOW IT'S THE RIGHT SHAPE!

Clink clank
Is this right?
WHAT AN AWFUL COLOR ...
Heh heh heh...
AND NOW...
FZZZ!
Sulfuric Acid
Water
...and file like mad!
Just take your time...
Eep
?!
grnd grnd
FILING THIS TINY CURVE IS HARD!
Increasingly miniscule grains
Over 12 types!
Fine
Rough
Polishers
Files

I THINK I'M GETTING THE HANG OF IT!
GOOD. KEEP AT IT!
gwif
gwuf
WHO TAUGHT YOU CHASING, GODA?
Um...
I'M MOSTLY SELF-TAUGHT.
I also attended a few classes.
WHEN DID YOU FIRST LEARN?
SECOND YEAR IN JUNIOR HIGH.

I WANTED SOMETHING I COULD LOSE MYSELF IN.
EVERY-ONE HAS TIMES LIKE THAT, YOU KNOW?
AFTER HIS GRAND-FATHER DIED...
...THE WORK-SHOP CLOSED...
...AND THAT MOVIE WAS LIKE GODA'S EULOGY.
HE USED STOP-MOTION TO FILM A TIN ROBOT...

...AND BRING IT TO LIFE.
INVESTED WITH THE OLD MAN'S SOUL...
...IT TOOK FLIGHT INTO THE SKY!

The Hot Spring Sommelier Murder Mystery: The Crime with Steam!
Detective Kaneda Morning Mist
I RECOMMENDED HE ENTER IT IN THE CONTEST.
THE DEPTH OF ITS EMOTION WOULD SET IT APART...
...FROM ALL THOSE AMATEUR FILMS.
BUT...
Youngest Ever
Ryuji Goda
Amateur Cinema Grand Prix
BUT WHEN IT EARNED HIGH PRAISE...
"I EXPLOITED MY GRANDFATHER'S DEATH."

"I USED IT FOR MY OWN SUCCESS."
BUT...
OF COURSE ...
...NO ONE ELSE SAW IT THAT WAY...
...AND HE MUST HAVE KNOWN THAT.

HE SELF-DESTRUCTED.
METAL-WORKING ...
...MEANS LEARNING THE METAL'S CHARACTERISTICS...
...AND DRAWING THEM OUT.
IT'S JUST ME AND THE METAL...
...SO I'M ALWAYS ALONE ...
...AND CAN'T HURT ANYONE.
MAKING MOVIES IS BY NATURE AN EGOTISTICAL ENDEAVOR ...

That criticism was spot-on...

...BORN OF PRIDE AND A SENSE OF RESPONSIBILITY FOR YOUR CREATION.

IF YOU...

...WORRY ABOUT DISRESPECTING SOMETHING AND CARRY AROUND THAT REGRET...

...THEN YOU AREN'T CUT OUT FOR IT.

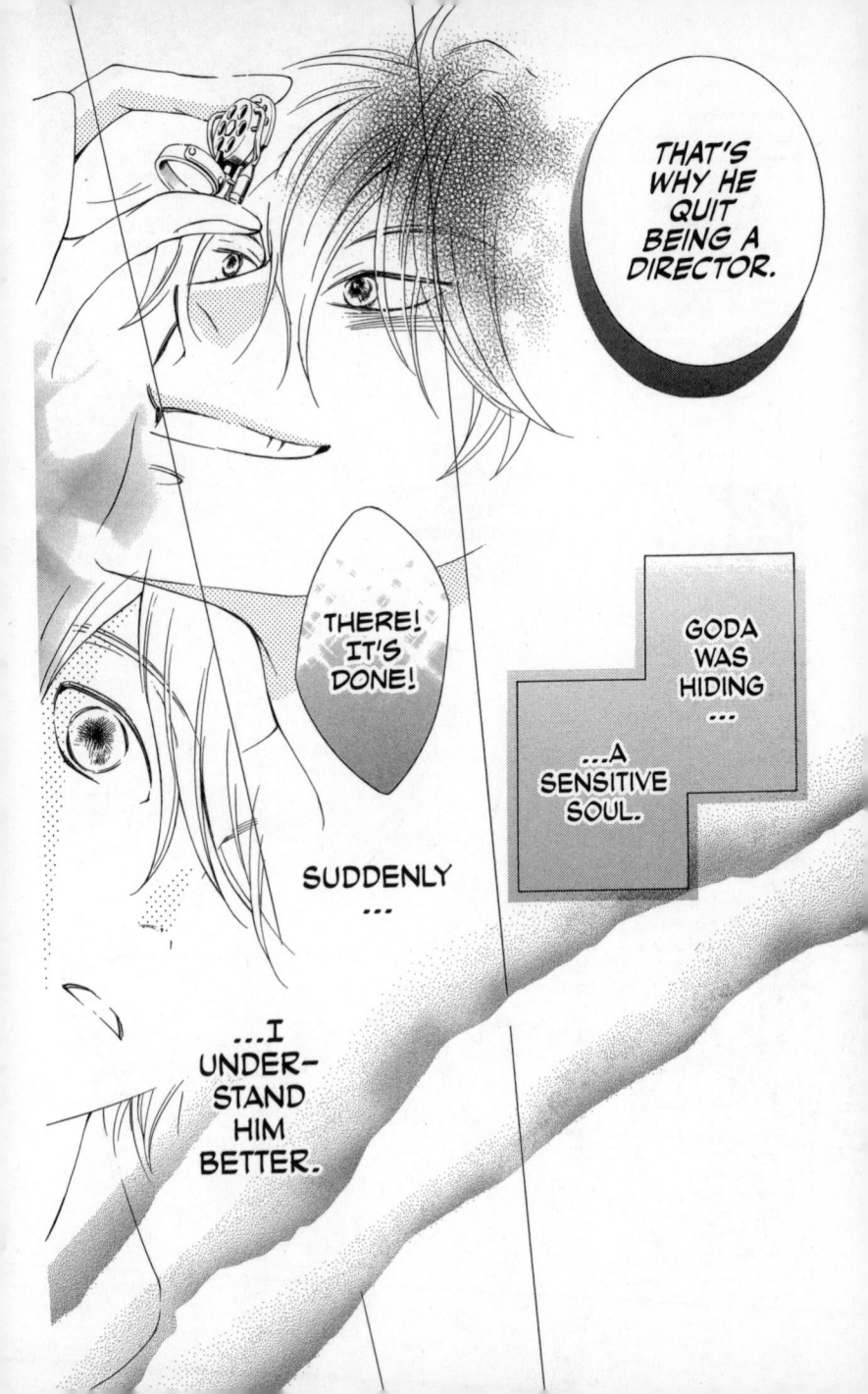
THAT'S WHY HE QUIT BEING A DIRECTOR.
THERE! IT'S DONE!
GODA WAS HIDING ...
...A SENSITIVE SOUL.
SUDDENLY ...
...I UNDER-STAND HIM BETTER.

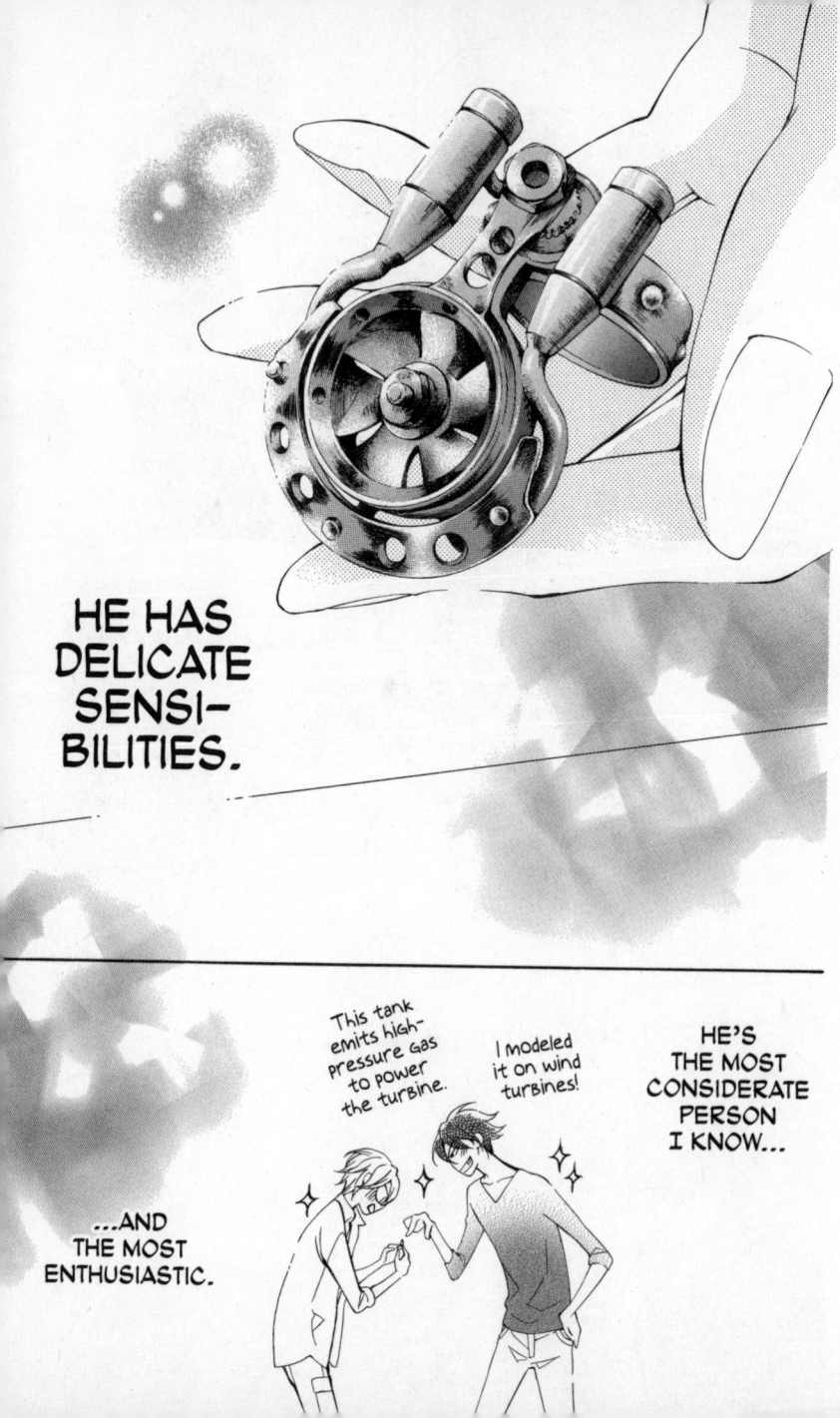
HE HAS DELICATE SENSI-BILITIES.
This tank emits high-pressure gas to power the turbine.
I modeled it on wind turbines!
HE'S THE MOST CONSIDERATE PERSON I KNOW...
...AND THE MOST ENTHUSIASTIC.

YOU'RE DONE?
I SEE YOU STAINED THE OUTSIDE WITH A BLACK DYE, THEN POLISHED THE INSIDE...
Oh!
NOT BAD FOR YOUR FIRST TIME!
...EVEN THOUGH YOU CAN'T SEE THAT WHEN YOU WEAR IT.
OH... IS THAT WEIRD?
Black Dye
Soaking it in a stain makes it look antique. ☆
NO, I LIKE IT!
IT'S KINDA LIKE YOU!

I'M STILL A BEGINNER WHEN IT COMES TO MOVIES...
...SO I DON'T KNOW ANY-THING.
BUT...
GODA ...
...ARE YOU...
...REALLY NEVER GOING TO DIRECT ANOTHER MOVIE?

HUH ...?
I WANT TO SEE...
... ANOTHER FILM BY YOU!!

SCENE
32

"I WANT TO SEE..."
"... ANOTHER FILM BY YOU!!"
HUH ?

WHAT'RE YOU—
Th...
THE OLD MAN IN THE TINPLATE FACTORY!
I KNOW HOW YOU FEEL!
I WOULD HAVE FELT THE SAME WAY!
"I EXPLOITED MY GRAND-FATHER'S DEATH."
BUT ...
"THAT'S WHY HE QUIT BEING A DIRECTOR."
...THAT MOVIE SPOKE TO ME!
YOU WEREN'T BEING DISRE-SPECT-FUL!
IT DIDN'T SEEM THAT WAY AT ALL!
SO DON'T BE HARD ON YOUR-SELF!
BE-CAUSE ...

...IT'S TOO SAD TO LIVE IN CONSTANT REGRET!
...
RE-GRET?
I'M NOT LIVING IN REGRET.
Sorry to break your flow, but...
WHAT ?!
BUT I HEARD THAT'S WHY YOU QUIT DIRECT-ING...
Not so loud...
OH, WAY BACK WHEN ?
...AND YOU'VE DRAGGED IT AROUND EVER SINCE!
UH... I HAVE?
HUH ?

What a coincidence!
ANYWAY, YOU SAW MY MOVIE?
IN FIFTH GRADE?
That blabber-mouth!
DID UICHIRO TELL YOU THAT?
?!
?!
?!
THAT WAS A TROUBLED TIME FOR ME...
...AND I DID STOP FILMING ...
...BUT THAT MOVIE WAS MY WAY OF MOURNING ...
...AND THE FAMILY APPRECI-ATED IT.
SO WHAT ABOUT NOW?
Actually...
I'M PROUD OF THAT MOVIE!
It's good, no?
Th...
THEN WHY DO YOU WORK BEHIND THE SCENES NOW?
Huh?
WELL, THAT'S BE-CAUSE ...
...that's where I've got major skills!

SO YOU DON'T WANT TO DIRECT ANY-MORE?
...
AT FIRST, PEOPLE JUST REQUESTED PROPS...
...BUT I HAD A BLAST WITH IT!
I GOT TO FLEX MY TALENT FOR CRAFTS ...
...AND SATISFYING REQUESTS IN MY OWN ORIGINAL WAY FELT GREAT!
No!
Abso-lutely not!!
SHO-CK

GLO-OM
WHAT A TOTAL ... WASTE OF EFFORT!
WAAA
Th...
AAA
AH
Gyargh!
I'm so embarrassed!
I just charged in all alone!
The likes of me presumed to encourage the great Goda!
Yeah...
THAT IS EMBARRASSING, BUT CALM DOWN!
I THOUGHT I HAD DRAWN CLOSER TO HIM ...
...BY LEARNING ABOUT HIS HIDDEN FRAGILITY.
IT THOUGHT HE WAS NO LONGER OUT OF REACH, BUT...
Reality
VWOOSH
WAIT!
SO ...

...ARE YOU JUST GOING TO GIVE UP?
YOU WANT TO SEE HIM...
...DIRECT A NEW MOVIE, RIGHT?
YEAH.
Hey...
RE-MEMBER THAT ONE TIME?
AT THE SCHOOL FESTI-VAL?
WHEN WE LEARNED IZUMI'S SECRET?
Shichiban University

BA
M
GODA ...
...LET'S MAKE A MOVIE!!
SF Club
Cinema Club
Film Stud
DA DOOM
DO WE HAVE TIME TO SPARE ?!
LOOK AT THIS BACK-BREAKING SCHEDULE !!
HUH ?!
WE ALREADY DIS-CUSSED THAT.
JUST ONCE!! JUST ONE MOVIE!
A...
A SHORT!! AND I'LL HELP!
NOW LISTEN HERE!

NO, UH...
Then let's combine projects to free up time!
SKRT SKRT SKRT
bing
SO YOUR ONLY OBJECTION IS SCHED-ULING?
Stop this nonsense and meet your quota!
HMM ---
I DON'T KNOW.
WHAT'S COME OVER RANMARU?
But this could be fun!!
Mwa ha
YOU'RE JUST USING THIS FOR YOUR OWN SELFISH PUR-POSES!
HERE'S AN IDEA! DO AN ACTION FLICK!!
I'VE GOT AN IDEA FOR PRINCESS ZAKURO'S SUCCESSOR!
MAKE YOUR COMEBACK WITH A GORY HORROR FILM!♡
Don't be so modest!
I SAW YOUR MOVIE TOO, CHIEF! ☆
RAN-MARU'S RIGHT! ♡

BUT THINK ABOUT IT.
WE DON'T HAVE THE NECESSARY MATERIALS.
Let's see... Glue and...
Oh?
NO PROBLEM! WE CAN BORROW FROM FILM STUDIES!
AND WHERE WOULD WE GET THE STAFF?
I EMAILED FURI AND SHE AGREED TO HELP!
How nice of her!
OKAAAAAY
I SAID I'M NOT DOING IT!
RANMARU! WHERE DID THIS CAN-DO SPIRIT COME FROM?!
Use it elsewhere!!
I'VE GOT A MEETING!
MEET YOUR QUOTAS OR ELSE!!
Later, let's strategize!!
Hurry! Hurry!!
SLAM

UM, RAN-MARU?
GODA DOESN'T WANT TO DO IT, SO...
I KNOW. BUT...
...I REALLY WANT TO SEE...
...A NEW MOVIE BY HIM!!
MY INSTINCTS TELL ME...
...IT'S TOO SOON TO GIVE UP, BUT...
"SO YOU DON'T WANT TO DIRECT ANY-MORE?"
...
MM
GODA!!
YOU CAN FILM MOVIES ON A SMART-PHONE NOW!!
BA
Tenba Motors

LISTEN, I'M NOT...
READY, TOMU?
AND... ACTION!
tok
tok
tok
tok
YEAH, I KNOW.
IT'S CHEAP AND EASY! PRETTY COOL, HUH?
WE SHOULD LOOK INTO THAT!
SOME HAVE EVEN WON ACADEMY AWARDS.
STAND IN THE LIGHT OVER THERE!
NICE! JUST LIKE A PICTURE!
MARVEL-OUS!! AND INNOVA-TIVE!!
RUN!! JUMP!!
NOW THE CAMERA PANS AND—
DON'T PAN BY SLINGING AROUND YOUR ARMS !!
BAA

USE AIR-PLANE MODE SO CALLS DON'T INTER-RUPT!
AND LOCK AE/AF! AUTOMATIC ADJUST-MENTS WILL JUST MESS IT UP!
Gasp
bamp
bamp
AND YOU'RE HOLDING IT WRONG!
DON'T USE ZOOM! TUCK IN YOUR ELBOWS !!
ON THE BIG SCREEN, THAT'D BE SHAKING ALL OVER!!
Correct
The Home button should be on the right.
Now back to work!!
EVEN WITH A NEW PASSION ...
...COULD HE FORGET A THING LIKE THAT?
SCHOOL CAFETERIA
GODA, HAVE YOU SEEN THIS MOVIE?
Yeah. I SAW THAT!
THE FRAM-ING IS GENIUS!
IT'S PER-FECTLY OFF-KILTER!
AND WHEN THE PILLARS DIVIDE THE FRAME, I GET GOOSE BUMPS!
DOESN'T HIS HEART ...

...FEEL A THRILL?
DOESN'T AN IRRESISTIBLE URGE...
...WELL UP WITHIN HIM...
...WHEN HE SEES...
...THAT SIGHT?
"I WANT ..."
"...TO DIRECT ANOTHER FILM."

SNARL
Gyaah!
I met my quota a day early!
DOES HE LACK THE TIME?
OR THE RIGHT OCCASION?
All-Nighter
Good. Here's more work.
Thump
Gyaah
OR...
This sunset is begging you to film it!
And check out this action!!
Use this gore I made, Chief!

Let's Watch Movies! 4
I made my horror-and-zombie flick debut!!!
Gyah!
Cushion
Eeeek!
Yikes!
I was noisier than the movie.
It makes sense, but gross-out flicks have a lot of blood.
It was terrifying.
However...
...was excellent!
Romero's Dawn of the Dead...
And the music and visuals came together splendidly!
The structure of the opening sequence and the use of color were awesome!
I watched the Dario Argento version.
AFTER ALL, GODA IS...
Wheew
Huff
I'M EXHAUSTED!

...
Oh, thanks.
Cafe
HAS AN ALIEN POS-SESSED HIM?
WAS HE ALWAYS LIKE THIS?
UGH ...
WHERE'S RAN-MARU?

AREN'T YOU TWO...
...GO-ING TO BUG ME TOO?
HA HA! DO YOU WANT US TO?
NO, DON'T.
AH HA HA!

IT'S BETTER NOT...
...TO FORCE THIS KIND OF THING.
YEAH ...
...A FILM IS QUITE AN UNDER-TAKING.
ARE YOU SAY-ING THAT ...

...BECAUSE IT'S PERSONAL FOR ME?
OR ARE YOU JUST BEING NICE?
OR...
...DO YOU THINK YOU DON'T HAVE THE RIGHT TO SPEAK UP?

BWAM
I FOUND THE CHIEF!!
RAN-MARU!! MAASA !!
Shut up!!!
I found a new contest for amateurs!
Are we playing tag?!
WHOOM
HUFF
I UNDER-STAND HOW RANMARU FEELS, THOUGH.
ME TOO.
LISTEN, GUYS...
Wait, Chief! I'll give you gum!
I don't want any!
...

KNOCK IT OFF, WILL YA?!
AM I DOING A BAD JOB IN THE ART SQUAD OR SOMETHING?
Stop harassing me!
NO, THAT'S NOT THE ISSUE.
THEN WHAT—
GODA ...

...YOU HAVE THE ABILITY TO TOUCH OTHERS.

I WAS NEVER COMFORTABLE ANYWHERE ...
...BUT THEN...
AMATEUR CINEMA CONTEST ENTRIES

...I REAL-IZED...
...THE WORLD IS A BIG PLACE.
SO THERE MUST BE...
...A PLACE FOR ME SOME-WHERE.

EVERY-THING CAME TOGETHER...
...WHEN I FOUND OUT WHO MADE THAT MOVIE.
SO NO MATTER WHAT...
...I WANT TO SEE...

...WHAT KIND OF MOVIE...
...THAT GUY WILL MAKE NOW.
LISTEN...
LIKE I SAID BEFORE...
EVEN IF I HAD A GREAT PERSONALITY...
...PERSONALITY DOESN'T MAKE MOVIES...
...AND NEITHER DOES KNOWLEDGE ABOUT MOVIES.
I KNOW THAT!
BUT YOU ACTUALLY MADE A GREAT MOVIE!
BUT...

...WHAT IF MY TALENT HAS DRIED UP?!
WHAT IF I MADE ANOTHER MOVIE...
...AND IT WAS UNWATCH-ABLE?!
THEN WHAT WOULD BE THE POINT OF GETTING OVER THE PAST?!
HUH?

UM...
...DOES THAT MEAN...
Gasp
SO...
ARE YOU...
...SO AGAINST THIS...

...because you're scared?

...
WHY, YOU ...

STOP RIGHT THERE, YOU !!!
WHOO
BINGO !!!
UH-OH!
I CAN'T BELIEVE IT!

There, there...
CHIEF ...
SHUT UP!
pat pat
GODA ...
...ALWAYS SEEMED SO OUT OF REACH, BUT...
Heh
NO WAY...

BWA HA HA HA
THIS IS GREAT!
"IF YOU'RE SERIOUS ABOUT THEM...
...YOU'LL DRAG THEM DOWN!!"
I am so...
HA HA HA HA
...gonna win this fight!!

SCENE 33

GODA!

DID YOU SAY...

...YOU WANT ME TO BRAIN-STORM IDEAS FOR YOUR MOVIE?

...

Blank

Behind the Scenes!!

Volume 7 is the last one!! Don't miss it!

I've already put everyone on the covers, so I'm overcome with emotion! What should I do for the last one?!

Thanks for the letters!

Bisco Hatori c/o
Lala Magazine, Hakusensha

2-2-2 Kanda-Awajicho
Chiyoda-ku
Tokyo, Japan
101-0063

NO, I DID NOT.
I DON'T HAVE A FILM.
fwip
ANYWAY, IF YOU'RE SHORT ON IDEAS, YOU CAN PICK FROM THESE!
fwip
MAASA HAS INSPIRATION FOR A SPLATTER FLICK...
...AND THE SF MOVIE CLUB WOULD PROBABLY HELP OUT!
HEY, DON'T JUST ...
Is this a presentation?!
AND FILM STUDIES HAD THREE SCRIPTS IN STOCK.
SUSPENSE, COMEDY AND A TEEN DRAMA!
RANMARU...
BUT DON'T WORRY!
THIS IS YOUR REHABILITATION FLICK, SO I MADE THEM PROMISE NOT TO BE OVERLY CRITICAL OF IT!
blah
blah
HUH...?
YOU DIDN'T TELL THEM ABOUT MY SITUATION, DID YOU?
YOUR SITUATION?

STAB
STAB
STAB
...BUT YOU ALSO HAVE A SIDE THAT'S SHAMELESSLY UNCOOL?
AND HOW YOU'RE ALWAYS SO SELF-RIGHTEOUS ...
...BUT YOU WERE ACTUALLY JUST SCARED AND PITIFUL?
YOU MEAN HOW YOU PRETENDED TO BE SENSITIVE AND TRAUMATIZED...
DA DU M
DO YOU THINK YOU'RE BETTER THAN US?!
AND MODEST. WHY HIDE THAT YOU WERE THE YOUNGEST TO WIN THAT CONTEST?
GODA, YOU'RE SO SECRETIVE.
Yep! I told 'em! ☆
W...

Want my pudding?
C'MON, CHEER UP, GODA!
I'M SO DISAPPOINTED...
...
!!
Snicker
Snicker
Oops. Never mind.
HE'S TALL, BUT WHAT A SCAREDY—
IT'S SO UNCOOL. I MEAN "SENSITIVE"!
WHEN I HEARD ABOUT YOUR SITUATION...
Now you lack credibility.
YOU TALK BIG, BUT...
Haneike, Film Studies, Year 1
Pssst
Is that why he's tall?
And he drinks Milo!
He's a BIG scaredy-cat!
It's because of his past.
I heard he wept like a baby.
YOU'RE THE DEVIL!
...SPREADING TRUTH AND FICTION! ☆
I LAUNCHED AN ALL-OUT OFFENSIVE ...
Heh heh...
Pssst

Heh
I've decided ...
...to be totally impolite !!
...
WHO ARE YOU ...?
WHAT HAVE YOU BE-COME ?!
BWA HA HA HA HA HA
Were you hiding this personality the whole time ?!
"I REALLY WANT TO SEE...
...A NEW MOVIE BY HIM"!

RANMARU PLOWED AHEAD UNSCRUPULOUSLY...
...IN ORDER TO DRAW OUT GODA'S TRUE FEELINGS.
BUT I...
"GODA DOESN'T WANT TO DO IT, SO..."
"IF GODA DOESN'T WANT US TO KNOW, THEN..."
"IT'S BETTER NOT TO FORCE THIS KIND OF THING."
I'M RUKA ENJOJI. I'M 21 YEARS OLD...
GLOOM
REGRET
...AND I'M WAY TOO GOOD AT BEING POLITE.

I WAS CLASS REPRE-SENTATIVE SIX TIMES.
I don't wanna be class rep!
Me neither!
I HELPED MY TEACHERS ...
...CLEAN PLACES NO ONE ELSE WOULD TOUCH.
IT'S IN MY NATURE TO STEP UP AND HANDLE THINGS.
AFTER MY MOTHER DIED...
...AND MY FATHER REMAR-RIED...
...AND I HAD TO LIVE WITH MY FAMILY'S DEMANDS...
...I THOUGHT THERE WAS NOTHING I COULD DO ABOUT IT.
"THIS IS MY FATE."
DID I GIVE UP?
ACTUALLY, I HAD ALREADY DECIDED...
SEE? ISN'T THAT A POSITIVE ATTITUDE?
Enjoji
RUKA ...

...HOW IS UNIVERSITY?
UM ...
...I LIKE IT!
THAT'S GOOD.

I KNOW!

IT WAS THE ONLY THING YOU ASKED FOR...
...BUT THE FAMILY IS ASKING ABOUT YOUR MARRIAGE PLANS.

THANKS, DAD!
AFTER GRADUATION, OKAY?
...
CHOOSING A REGULAR UNIVERSITY INSTEAD OF A SCHOOL FOR RICH KIDS...
...WAS MY FIRST AND LAST ADVENTURE.
HEY...
Chatter
Chatter
Aichan University

...I HEARD YOU'RE GOOD AT SEWING.
CAN YOU LEND ME A HAND?
53
THE LEAD ACTRESS AND THIS DOLL NEED THE SAME DRESS?
Huh?! Who told you that?!
A GIRL IN MY CLASS.
YOU ADJUSTED HER SKIRT.
B-b-but—
FILM STUDIES WANTS PROPS AND I CAN'T DO EVERYTHING MYSELF!
YANK
YANK
YEAH.
FINDING FABRIC TO MATCH A STORE-BOUGHT DRESS IS HARD...
...SO IT WOULD BE FASTER TO JUST MAKE BOTH.

Yeah...
CAN YOU DO IT?
WHAT'S THE BUDGET AND DEAD-LINE?
IT SHOULDN'T BE TOO HARD TO MAKE A SIMPLE ONE-PIECE...
...LIKE THIS ONE, BUT–
HUH?
YOU MADE THAT YOUR-SELF?!
Aha!!
I CAN HIGHLIGHT THE SIMILARITY BY USING THE SAME RIBBON!
I'VE GOT THE PERFECT FABRIC AT HOME!
Yeah.
I'D APPRE-CIATE IT.
Sparkle
Sparkle
BUT I CAN'T PAY YOU.
HM?
WHAT'S THAT BOX?
I MADE THAT DURING SOME FREE TIME.
IT'S SO SMOOTH !!
AND THE EDGES ARE SO PRECISE !!
What wonderful right angles!!
Can I have this?!

That's weird!
Huh? Right angles?
GACK
heh
Heh heh
AHH ...
GRIN
THAT'S RIGHT!
GLORIOUS RIGHT ANGLES !!
THEY'RE A PERFECT 90 DEGREES!!
MORE THAN PRECISE, THEY'VE GOT CHARACTER!
YEAH! UH-HUH!
IT HIT ME LIKE A FLASH.

All done?
Nice to meet you!
I found another helper!
He was sketching out back!
BRIL-LIANCE ...
... PASSION ...
...AND ENVY...
YOU'RE AMAZING ...
AND THEN ...
Oh, wow!
Um, are you the Ryuji Goda who...

I'LL PUT ALL THESE FEELINGS...
...IN A BOX.
WE SHARED OUR ENTHU-SIASM...
...AND EVERYONE GAVE ME COURAGE...

...AND I LEARNED TO LIKE MYSELF.
AREN'T YOU TWO...
...GOING TO BUG ME TOO?
ARE YOU JUST BEING NICE?
OR...
...DO YOU THINK YOU DON'T HAVE THE RIGHT TO SPEAK UP?
BUT THEN...
...HE MADE ME REALIZE SOMETHING.
I...

I LACK PRIDE IN MYSELF.

I PRETEND I HAVE A DUTY TO FULFILL...

...BUT THAT'S A LIE.

I also wanted to talk about Japanese films, but...

Heh
MAASA...
IT MUST BE NICE TO BE SO DESIRABLE...
Handsome Dude Contest
THAT OBLIVIOUS MYSTERIOUSNESS MAKES US TINGLE!
The Handsome Dude Contest
SHICHIKOKU Handsome Dude Contest
THERE'S ACTUALLY A CONTEST?
I had no idea!
I did?
Fill in this survey!
YOU'RE GONNA LOOK FOR A JOB?
Huh?
YES, OF COURSE!
Shall we eat together?
GOING TO LUNCH?
Uh...
SORRY, I HAVE A JOB-HUNTING SEMINAR.
YOUR FAMILY IS RICH, RUKA...
...BUT WHAT ABOUT THOSE OTHER TWO?
HMM...
They're staying for a fifth year?!
They spent too much time on movies.
TCH! FILM FREAKS...
AH HA HA!
IT'S STRANGE THAT YOU GUYS AREN'T!!
No one else...
Laid back
...is bothering.
ANYWAY, DID YOU HEAR ABOUT RIICHI AND UICHIRO?

...I DON'T KNOW.
I'M SO CLOSE, BUT...
...I CAN'T TAKE A STEP FORWARD.
SH
G-GODA ?!
Godaaaaa!
OH! RUKA!
WHAT ARE YOU DO-ING?
RAN-MARU'S AFTER ME.
UH-OH!
CLIMB ON!!
HUH ?!
SCREECH

JUST GET ON!!
Ranmaru?!
CHIEEEF!!!
Kyaaah!!!
HOLD ON!!!
TROMMP

Creak
Creak
Creak
Creak
On campus
He got away...
Wheezy Huff
Too slow.

WELL, HE'S SERIOUS ABOUT THIS.
Chucky
A scary doll in horror movies
BUT I NEED TIME FOR INSPIRATION!
THAT GUY SCARES ME! HE'S STARTING TO LOOK LIKE CHUCKY!
DID YOU LOSE HIM?

EVERY-ONE ALREADY THINKS I'M UNCOOL ...
...AND IF IT WEREN'T FOR THIS...
...I MIGHT NEVER MOVE FORWARD.
I SUP-POSE.
ARE YOU GOING TO DIRECT A MOVIE?

THE DESIRE WAS ALWAYS THERE IN THE BACK-GROUND.
BUT ...
...I HAVEN'T FOUND THE RIGHT SUBJECT MATTER YET.
WOW ...
RANMARU HAD AN EFFECT ON YOU.
I WISH I DID!
Tee hee! ☆
WHAT ?!
YOU'VE HAD A MAJOR EFFECT ON ME!
HUH ?!
YOU TOLD ME ABOUT...
...THAT MIND-BLOWING BEEF BOWL ...
...AT THAT ONE DINER!
STAB

FWEEEE
I'VE NEVER KNOWN A GIRL SO CRAZY ABOUT MEAT!
AND YOU'VE GOT STRONG ARMS!
MEAT MUST BRING OUT YOUR POTEN-TIAL!
OKAY. ENOUGH ABOUT MEAT.
EEE
I LOVE HOW YOU LIKE RIGHT ANGLES ...
...AND KNOW HOW TO PERSE-VERE!
YOU GRIT YOUR TEETH...
...AND KEEP ON SMILING!
SO DON'T ACT...
...LIKE EVERYONE ELSE IS SO SUPER-HUMAN.
GODA ...

IT HAS BEEN MY SALVATION ...
...TO HAVE YOU SMILING BY MY SIDE.
UH-OH...

I LIKE HIM SO MUCH...
...THAT I CAN'T HOLD IT INSIDE ANYMORE.
HUG
GYAH ?!

Swerve
W-WHAT'RE YOU DOING THAT FOR ?!
Kyah!
S-SORRY!
Radio waves!
Mysterious waves from outer space!!
Um... I JUST, UM...
WHAT?! FROM SPACE ?!
Y-yeah!! They hit my brain and ordered me to do it!!
SERIOUSLY ?!
I'LL GET OFF NOW.
S-SORRY ...

WELL, IF RADIO WAVES MADE YOU DO IT...
...THEN KEEP OBEYING THEM.

WHERE CAN I...
...KEEP ALL THESE FEEL-INGS?
SHALL WE GO GET A BEEF BOWL?
HEY, GOOD IDEA!
When we get off campus, hop off.
SHICHIKOKU PARK

IZUMI?
SOH! LONG TIME NO SEE!
THIS KITTY'S NAP-PING, SO I CAN'T MOVE.
PURR
PURR
IT'S SO CUTE!
I THOUGHT HE WAS CRYING...
Phew!
WHAT'S THAT?
IT'S SOME KIND OF SURVEY...
Shichikoku Handsome Dude Contest
Q1 What were you like as a child?
Q2 What was your dream as a child?
Q3 Who was your favorite celebrity as a
Q4 What junior high clubs were yo
Q5 When was your first love?
have you changed since
ur dream now?
I'M SUR-PRISED...
...AT HOW FEW ANSWERS I HAVE.
THE OLDER STUDENTS...

BEHIND THE SCENES!! VOLUME 6 – THE END

Bonus Manga
Sci-fi Club!!
SCHOOL CAFETERIA
Annoud
CALLING ALL MEMBERS!
THIS IS THE PRESIDENT!
TODAY'S LUNCH IS HAM CUTLET!
tunk
Meat udon
Chicken nanban
Fried meat
This is the Sci-fi Movie Club.
Their dream is to be telepathic. ☆
The End
whisper
whisper
whisper
MAYBE THERE WAS ELECTRO-MAGNETIC INTERFERENCE!
NO, BOYS ALWAYS GET MEAT, SO...
BUT WE ALL GOT MEAT, SO IT SORT OF COUNTS ...?
ARGH! IT DIDN'T WORK AGAIN!

Bonus Manga
Sci-fi Club 2!!
THIS IS AN URGENT MATTER.
WE SHOULD GO BY A SPATIAL CURVATURE WARP.
Clubroom
NO, I RECOMMEND A NORMAL PROPULSION WARP.
YOUR THEORIES ARE TOO RECK-LESS!
MORE SPEED, LESS HASTE, BRO!
I'LL JUST GO THE USUAL WAY.
VERY WELL. GOOD LUCK TO ALL!
GRAA
And off they went to get the cafeteria pudding before it ran out!!!
Cafe-teria
Wing 2
Wing 1
Club Wing
Main Bldg.
Wing 3
AAA
This pudding's awesome!
Wheez
Wheew
TOM
They all lost.
Warp Theory = Shortcut
H

Special Thanks!

★Nakajima-sama
★Okazaki-sama
★Everyone on the editorial staff
★Everyone involved in publishing this book

★Jewelry Forêt
Jho-sama / Michiko-sama

★Takashi Iwabuchi-sama

★Yajima-sama

★Staff:
Yui Natsuki / Aya Aomura / Shizuru Onda / Umeko / Keiko / Miki Namiki / Shii Tsunokawa

Meiji-sama
Haruka Chino-sama

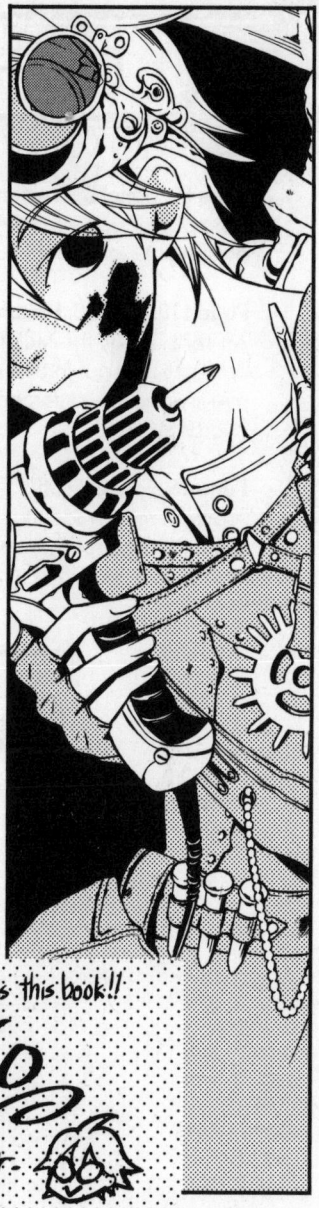

And everyone who reads this book!!

Bisco

2018.Mar.

GLOSSARY

Page 50, panel 2: Koshien
A stadium in Japan, and the usual site of a prestigious high school baseball tournament.

Page 110, panel 6: Haitorei Edict
An 1876 act by the Meiji government that prohibited all but former daimyo lords, the military and law enforcement from carrying swords in public.

Page 159, panel 5: Milo
A powdered chocolate malt drink for kids popular in the southern hemisphere and Japan.

AUTHOR BIO

Pieces by Forêt-sama have appeared in the manga. This time, I made the simple ring above.

-Bisco Hatori

Bisco Hatori made her manga debut with ***Isshun kan no Romance*** (**A Moment of Romance**) in ***LaLa DX*** magazine. The comedy ***Ouran High School Host Club*** was her breakout hit and was published in English by VIZ Media. Her other works include ***Detarame Mousouryoku Opera*** (Sloppy Vaporous Opera), ***Petite Pêche!*** and the vampire romance ***Millennium Snow***, which was also published in English by VIZ Media.

Behind the Scenes!!

VOLUME 6

Shojo Beat Edition

STORY AND ART BY **Bisco Hatori**

English Translation & Adaptation/John Werry
Touch-Up Art & Lettering/Sabrina Heep
Design/J. Shikuma
Editor/Pancha Diaz

Urakata!! by Bisco Hatori
© Bisco Hatori 2018
All rights reserved.
First published in Japan in 2018 by HAKUSENSHA, Inc., Tokyo.
English language translation rights arranged with HAKUSENSHA, Inc., Tokyo.

The stories, characters and incidents mentioned in this publication are entirely fictional.

No portion of this book may be reproduced or transmitted in any form or by any means without written permission from the copyright holders.

Printed in the U.S.A.

Published by VIZ Media, LLC
P.O. Box 77010
San Francisco, CA 94107

10 9 8 7 6 5 4 3 2 1
First printing, March 2019

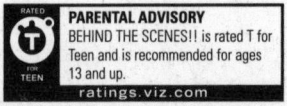

www.viz.com

www.shojobeat.com

From the creator of *Ouran High School Host Club!*

Millennium Snow™

By Bisco Hatori

Seventeen-year-old Chiyuki has heart problems, and her doctors say she won't live to see the next snow. Touya is a young vampire who hates blood and refuses to make the traditional partnership with a human, whose life-giving blood would keep them both alive for a thousand years. Can Chiyuki teach Touya to feel a passion for life, even as her own is ending?

Only $9.99

Shojo Beat
MANGA from the HEART

www.shojobeat.com

Also available at your local bookstore and comic store.

Sennen no Yuki © Bisco Hatori 1998/HAKUSENSHA, Inc.

ratings.viz.com

Shojo Beat

viz media
www.viz.com

YOU MAY BE READING THE WRONG WAY!

This book reads from right to left to maintain the original presentation and art of the Japanese edition, so action, sound effects and word balloons are reversed. This diagram shows how to follow the panels. Turn to the other side of the book to begin.